THE KINDNESS BOOMERANG

Hawys Morgan

Illustrated by **Tika and Tata**

OXFORD
UNIVERSITY PRESS

Letter from the Author

When I think about kindness, I remember my first day at secondary school. The desks in our new classroom were in pairs. I found a seat and sat down. A girl I didn't know walked up to me and said, 'Hi, I'm Rebecca. Is anyone sitting here?'

I wanted to save the seat for my friend Lisa, who wasn't at school that day. I replied, 'Sorry, it's taken.' Rebecca walked away sadly. I regretted it at once. Rebecca was new and didn't know anybody at the school. I should have been kinder.

I vowed to be more welcoming from then on.

Over the following years, Rebecca and I became best friends. In fact, we're still best friends now!

As an adult, I try to be kind. It costs nothing to smile at your neighbour, or to hold open the door for someone at the shop – but things like that can make everyone a little bit happier.

Hawys Morgan

Contents

What Does Kindness Feel Like? 4

The Science behind Kindness 6

Fabulous Friends 10

Everyone is Unkind Sometimes 14

Be Kind to Yourself 23

Random Acts of Kindness 27

Glossary 31

Index 32

The glossary

Some words in this book are in **bold**. When you read a **bold** word, think about what it means. If you don't know, you can look it up in the glossary at the end of the book.

What Does Kindness Feel Like?

Think about the last time someone was kind to you. Did you feel any of these **emotions**?

happiness

warmth

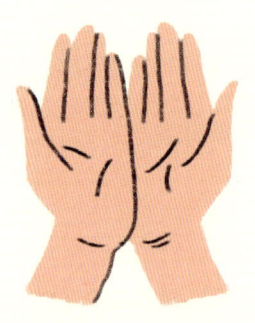

gratitude

safety

inclusion

Now think about the last time you were kind to somebody else. What emotions did you feel?

Many people feel even happier when they are the person *being* kind. Like a **boomerang**, the **positive** emotions you give come back to you.

kindness

happiness

The Science behind Kindness

When you are kind, your body releases chemicals that make you feel good.

The cuddle chemical

Have you ever felt a kind of 'warm glow' after doing something kind? That warm glow is caused by a chemical called **oxytocin** (*say* ox-ee-toa-sin). Your body produces oxytocin when you are kind to someone or when you are close to them. Oxytocin is sometimes called the 'cuddle chemical'.

It makes you feel good in several ways:

- You feel more relaxed.
- You feel more positive.
- It increases your **self-confidence**.
- You feel more affectionate.

Puppy love

Some animals' bodies produce oxytocin, too. Scientists measured oxytocin levels in pet dogs. They discovered that the dogs produced a burst of oxytocin when they made eye contact with their owners.

It's not just pets that benefit from oxytocin. In experiments, scientists gave extra oxytocin to seals and meerkats (this didn't harm them). Thanks to the oxytocin, these wild animals became friendlier and fought less.

The happy chemical

When you are kind, part of your brain becomes active and releases a chemical called **dopamine** (*say* doa-pa-meen). Dopamine makes you feel happy. So the kinder you are, the better you feel.

Did you know?

Your dopamine levels also rise when you:

- exercise
- laugh
- listen to music.

Fabulous Friends

Friendship is a wonderful thing that can make us feel great. Good friends are kind to each other. How can you be a kind friend?

Be there

Is one of your friends acting a little differently? Do they seem worried or sad? Sometimes the kindest thing you can do for a friend is just be there.

Each friend is different, so how you support them will be different too. It might mean listening to their worries or giving them a hug. It might mean baking a cake or playing football with them. Whatever it is, make sure your friends know you are there for them.

Making up

It's normal to argue with friends sometimes. When it happens, it can feel like your world is falling apart. Ignoring the problem won't make it go away, but talking about it might help.

Try telling your friend how you feel. Remember to ask your friend how *they* feel, too. If you think you may have acted unfairly, say sorry.

I'm sorry.

It can take courage to take the first step in making up, but you'll feel better for trying.

Making new friends

There are all sorts of reasons why people become friends. You may be friends with one person because you both like swimming. Somebody else might be your friend because they make you laugh. Why not try to find something in common with somebody new? It could be as simple as you both liking the same song.

Your new best friend might be right in front of you – you just don't know it yet!

Everyone is Unkind Sometimes

If you look up 'kindness' in the dictionary, you might read something like this:

kindness (noun): being friendly and generous

That sounds easy! But *is* it easy to be kind all the time?

Do you ever say things like this?

You can't play with us.

Your lunch looks disgusting.

You can't sit here.

It's mine – you can't have it.

You're rubbish at this.

I don't care what you think.

If you do say things like that, you're certainly not the only one. Everyone is unkind sometimes. Nobody is perfect. There are lots of reasons why people can be unkind. Understanding those reasons can help us learn how to be kinder.

Angry emotions

When we feel angry, it's easy to say something we don't mean. Here are a few warning signs that you might be about to explode:

Red face

Clenching your teeth

Heart beating quickly

Feeling sick

They're only some of the things people feel when they're angry. Other people may feel different things, or not know how they feel.

16

How can you avoid losing your temper and saying something unkind?

In the moment, you could try:

o slowly breathing in and out while counting to ten

o walking away

o talking about your feelings.

Later, you could try:

o getting some fresh air

o listening to relaxing music

o shaking out those cross feelings by exercising or dancing

o having a nap.

It can be helpful to work out why you are feeling angry, but it isn't easy to do.

Sometimes we feel angry because we are worried, scared, lonely, tired or jealous. Even feeling hungry can sometimes make you feel grumpy!

Everyone feels angry sometimes. It's part of being human. It's OK to feel angry if something is wrong or unfair. Anger can help us to make positive changes.

FACT FILE | Greta Thunberg

Greta Thunberg

Greta first learned about **climate change** when she was eight. She could not understand why people didn't want to protect the planet. It made her angry! That anger changed her life. She started **protesting** against the causes of climate change. Soon, thousands of children across the world were protesting with her.

Copycat

We often copy how people around us act. If a friend is laughing, it can make us laugh too – even when we don't know what the joke is! If you smile at someone, they will often smile back.

It's the same for **negative** feelings: if you are mean to someone, they could be mean back.

If someone is being unkind, try to take a step back and think about that person's life. Maybe they have lost someone or something they love. Perhaps they are worried about school or their family. They may think that everything in your life seems easy and feel jealous of you.

When sad or difficult things happen, it can be hard to know how to cope. Life can feel unfair. It can make people lash out in a mean way, and they might do things they then regret.

If you feel safe, try reaching out to those who are unkind. You might be surprised and see a different side to them. Maybe they need a little kindness themselves. You could reach out by simply asking:

Are you OK?

If someone is often unkind and won't listen to you, you should tell a grown-up that you trust.

Be Kind to Yourself

It's important to be kind to others, but it's important to be kind to yourself too. Being kind to yourself improves your wellbeing, which means being comfortable, happy and healthy. There are some things we can do to improve our wellbeing.

A healthy body, a healthy mind

Have you ever heard the expression 'a healthy body, a healthy mind'? It means that our bodies and our minds are connected. If your body is healthy, it helps your **mental** health. In the same way, if your mental health is good, it can help your **physical** health.

Healthy body:
- exercise
- get enough sleep
- eat and drink well.

Healthy mind:
- see your friends
- do activities you love
- talk about your feelings
- be thankful for the good things in life.

It's OK to make mistakes

Sometimes we can give ourselves a hard time when we make mistakes – but making mistakes is a part of life, and it can help us learn.

When you have negative thoughts about yourself, try to make those thoughts more positive.

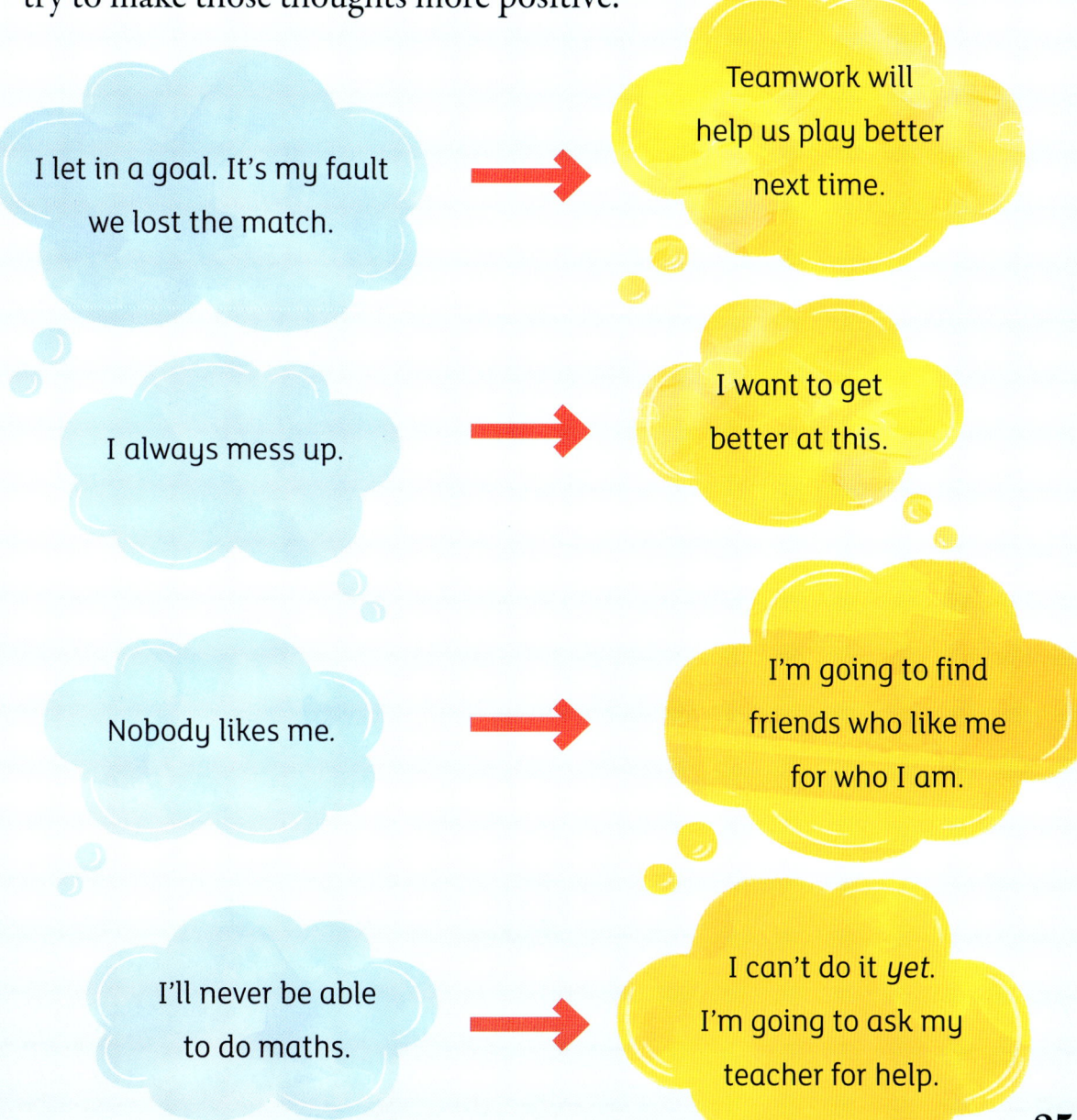

I let in a goal. It's my fault we lost the match. → Teamwork will help us play better next time.

I always mess up. → I want to get better at this.

Nobody likes me. → I'm going to find friends who like me for who I am.

I'll never be able to do maths. → I can't do it *yet*. I'm going to ask my teacher for help.

Remembering acts of kindness

- Find a jar, box or notebook and decorate it.
- When someone is kind to you or you are kind to someone else, write down what happened and how it makes you feel. Save it in the jar, box or notebook.
- If you're having a bad day, read one of the memories.

Random Acts of Kindness

Kindness is a choice. We can all choose to be kinder.

FACT FILE | Nicholas Lowinger

Nicholas Lowinger

When Nicholas Lowinger was a teenager, he met a brother and sister who were homeless. They took it in turns to go to school because they shared a single pair of shoes. Nicholas gave the brother a new pair of shoes, so he and his sister could *both* go to school every day.

This act of kindness changed the lives of the brother and sister. It changed Nicholas's life, too. He went on to set up a charity that gives thousands of pairs of new shoes to children in need.

Can you do one extra kind thing a day?

Five ways to be kind at school:

1. Smile at your classmates and your teacher.
2. Ask someone new to sit next to you.
3. Invite someone to play with you.
4. Give someone a **compliment**, such as 'I like your drawing.'
5. Hold open a door for someone.

Five ways to be kind at home:

1. Ask your parent or carer, 'Did you have a good day?'
2. Tidy up without being asked.
3. Let someone else in your family choose what game to play or what to watch on TV.
4. Help to carry the shopping.
5. Say thank you for meals.

Being kind to others invites others to be kind to you.
The kindness comes back – just like a BOOMERANG!

29

Remember

There are lots of ideas in this book for how to help yourself and others.

If you are worried about yourself or someone else, make sure you talk to an adult you trust.

Glossary

boomerang: a curved piece of wood that can come back to the person who throws it

clenching: closing tightly

climate change: a change in weather over a long time

compliment: an expression of approval or praise

dopamine: a chemical made by your body that can help you to feel happy and relaxed

emotions: strong feelings

gratitude: noticing what is good in our lives and being thankful

inclusion: including and welcoming someone as part of a group

mental: to do with the mind

negative: to be gloomy and critical

oxytocin: a chemical made by your body that makes you feel happy and affectionate

physical: to do with the body

positive: to be hopeful and upbeat

protesting: showing seriously that you disagree with something

self-confidence: belief in your own abilities

Index

angry 16–19

animals 7

argue 12

chemicals 6–9, 31

dopamine 8–9, 31

family 21, 29

friends 10–13, 24–25

Greta Thunberg 19

happiness 4–5, 8, 23

mistakes 25

Nicholas Lowinger 27

oxytocin 6–7, 31

talk 12, 17, 24, 30

Dead Good

written by Alan Brown

illustrated by Caroline Firenza

Preface

It's amazing what you can find out about people buried in graveyards and cemeteries.

When we started looking after gravestones and landscape in the Sheffield General Cemetery we only knew about a handful of people buried there, most of them the grand men of Victorian Sheffield, like Mark Firth, who was a big name in the Sheffield steel industry.

More exciting was discovering that many of the ordinary people buried in the cemetery turned out not to be so ordinary after all: like the man who gathered a crowd to watch him sail down the River Don in a wash tub pulled by ducks, and a baby from an Ashantee village that had been transported to Sheffield as a peep show – rather like today's TV show 'Big Brother' perhaps?

All the stories printed in this book are based on facts: they have just been re-written and developed from the information we had – usually newspaper articles – to make them more entertaining.

There are 87,000 people buried in the Sheffield General Cemetery: just think how many more stories there are to discover.

Why not visit your nearest graveyard or cemetery and see what interesting information you can find on the gravestones? Let your imagination do the rest! Meanwhile, enjoy this small selection of stories and the lovely illustrations.

Body Snatchers!

The body's got ter be fresh, yer know. Yer can't get a good price for any old stinkin' corpse! A boy or gel that's not bin in the ground more than a week, that's best. Easier diggin' too. Well, I've got a bad back, yer know. Shouldn't be in this business at all, tell the truth. Diggin' em up in the dead of night, six feet down, sometimes. Not usually, though. Too many others down there! Gravediggers have to squash 'em up. Make room! Make room!

'Scuse me while I coff. Ah, that's better. Workin' out in the cold and the wet, that's the cause of it. And the liftin', don't forget the liftin'. 'Course, we don't get the coffin out, do we. Just wot's inside! Mind you, they don't weigh much. Thin wood. Cheap. They takes the brass off when the family's gone. Take the whole coffin, some undertakers do!

I should know. I'm an undertaker meself. Well, an assistant, one of them mutes wot walks alongside the hearse and looks all solemn. Sometimes I carry this here wand wot shows I'm guardin' the dear departed. Keepin 'em safe! That's a joke! 'Scuse me while I coff.

This is 'ow it works. The sawbones up the hill puts in an order. Doctors is always wanting bodies to cut up, them and their students. Dunno how they do it. Fair makes me flesh creep! Anyway, we tell 'im wots comin' and he takes his pick. Bury 'em in the day, dig 'em up at night. Over yer shoulder and hope the old Bill don't see yer. Cash on delivery at the side door of the surgery.

The cadaver don't complain. The doc gets wot he wants, my boss gets a cut for turnin' the proverbial blind eye, my missus gets the money to feed our little uns – and I get a bad back. Well, it's a livin'.

War and Peace

My name is Charles Partington. I was seventeen when I ran away with my friends to fight in the Crimea. We told the recruiting officer we were eighteen and he wasn't particular. We were eager to be heroes, me most of all.

Well, I'm getting a hero's send-off all right. Riding on a gun carriage with the Union Jack over my coffin and my helmet on top. There's crowds of people I don't know from Adam. I wonder who polished the helmet?

Could have been one of the veterans firing the salute. They're in full dress uniform, a bright splash of colour in the black. Easy targets for snipers, they'd be. Can't abide snipers. The cowards never fight you face to face.

I nearly copped it more than once. A cossack sword in my guts at Sebastopol, returned with interest. I was nursed by the Lady of the Lamp. A proper angel, was Florence Nightingale. The generals did their best to get us killed and she did her best to save us.

They ordered us to charge the guns at Balaklava. Cavalry against artillery! The Light Brigade was cut down like wheat. It was madness. Lucan ordered the Heavies to retreat or we would have gone down too. When we enlisted I never thought it would be like that. I was wet behind the ears, just a boy.

I was lucky to come out of the war alive, but my friends were all dead. You never get over a thing like that. I think of them every day, see their faces, forever young. In Sheffield I've tried to help the veterans who're broken and maimed, but it breaks your heart, how little you can do.

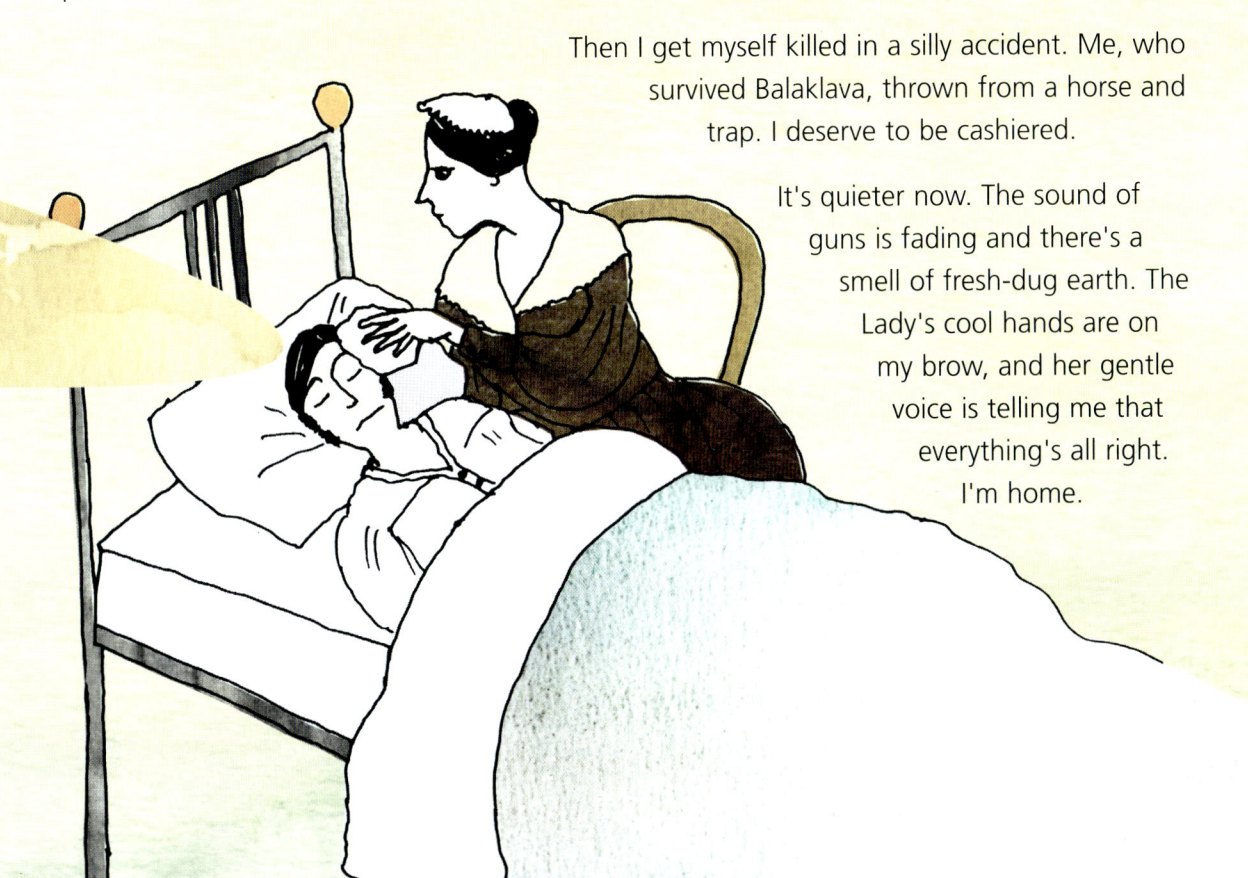

Then I get myself killed in a silly accident. Me, who survived Balaklava, thrown from a horse and trap. I deserve to be cashiered.

It's quieter now. The sound of guns is fading and there's a smell of fresh-dug earth. The Lady's cool hands are on my brow, and her gentle voice is telling me that everything's all right. I'm home.

The Monkey Man

Was he a man, or was he a beast? In early Victorian times, Harvey Teasdale was a great success in pantomimes, pretending to be a monkey!

Harvey was always very nimble and acrobatic. Once, he announced that he would sail down the River Don in a washing tub pulled by ducks. It was a stunt to get publicity for the comedy that he was appearing in at the theatre the same evening.

It worked! 70,000 people lined the river bank. The ducks pulled mightily, but when the tub was opposite Cocker's Wire Works disaster struck. There were so many people straining to see that a wall fell down and they tumbled into the river!

'The piercing shrieks that accompanied the fall might have appalled a stouter heart than mine, and made a sensation not easily shaken off. I remember seeing a pair of crutches appear above the water, and then going down, and an old woman rising, whose ghastly features were made more hideous by the way she screamed for help, and cursed old Harvey and his ducks. Thank God, no lives were lost.'

Lots of people came to the theatre, and Harvey put the ticket money in a clothes box. After the show, he and his wife staggered down the street with it. Disaster struck again!

The box burst and cash spilled out. Coins rolled down the road. Passers-by stuffed them in their pockets and walked away as fast as they could. Harvey didn't need a box for what was left.

The Monkey Man's life was full of ups and downs. He earned a lot as a monkey impersonator, but spent it on drink. His wife left him and he tried to shoot her. The judge sent him to Wakefield Prison.

Harvey was always a tearaway, but in prison a strange thing happened.

'Jesus showed me the error of my ways. He called me and I was saved. My life began anew. I gave up drinking. There will be no more conceit and foolishness on the stage. The rest of the time God allows me on this earth I devote to his service.'

Harvey Teasdale was allowed many more years, spending them as a shopkeeper and preacher. He died at the good age of 86.

Buried Alive!

There was a young man at Nunhead
Who awoke in his coffin of lead;
'It is cosy enough,'
He remarked, in a huff,
'But I wasn't aware I was dead.'

A weird illness has struck you down. You cannot move a muscle, but you see everything. A doctor bends over you, trying to find a faint heart-beat, a feather breath. A shadow falls across your face and all is dark. He has closed your eyes. He thinks you're dead.

Your parents are crying and you cannot comfort them. They love you more now than ever before.

The undertakers heave you around like a sack of coal. They do all sorts of disgusting things. You try to shout, 'I'm alive! You're hurting me!' No sound comes. You hear your mother say how beautiful you look, but you do not feel beautiful.

You hear a thud, and feel it through your body like a blow. They have closed the lid of your coffin.

The vicar is talking about you. This is your funeral. For once, you hope that he will speak for a long time, but he hardly knows you. All too soon you feel the coffin swaying gently as it is lowered into the fresh-dug grave.

You are going to be buried alive!

You want to scream, but you cannot open your mouth! You want to bang on the coffin, but you cannot lift your hand! You are completely paralysed!

Soil rattles down onto the coffin lid, just a handful at first, then a little more, and then great shovel loads. It becomes very quiet. Everyone has gone away.

In the almost total silence, you hear two things. One is the faint beating of your heart. The other is such slow, shallow breathing that it would hardly disturb a feather.

The Victorians took the danger of premature burial very seriously indeed. With good reason. Doctors did not know so much as they do now and there were many cases of 'dead' people reviving at the undertaker's or in the mortuary.

When the College of Surgeons opened some coffins in London, they found three people had been buried alive. How could the surgeons tell? Were there scratch marks as the victims tried frantically to claw their way out? Were their faces contorted as they suffocated in pain and terror?

There were a number of ways of tackling the problem of premature burial. One was to make quite sure that the person was dead. Cutting arteries or removing the heart was reckoned to be pretty effective. Waiting for the corpse to start decomposing before burying it was another safe bet.

A different approach was to give the corpse some means of saying, 'Hang on a bit! I'm still in the land of the living, thank you very much!'

Bells tied to the fingers of bodies in the mortuary rang at the slightest movement. The rich and nervous had Count Karnice-Karnicki's machine put in their grave. If they woke up after being buried alive, they could breathe through a tube and make a flag on a stick pop out of the ground. Let's hope somebody saw it!

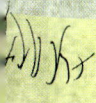

Samuel Holberry speaks from the coffin

There's 50,000 people turned out for my funeral. Not bad, for the son of a farm labourer, and a convicted criminal to boot. The Lord Mayor couldn't do better than that!

I can hear the racket from my coffin. There's a band leading the procession through the streets of Sheffield, boom, boom, boom. Next come my Chartist comrades marching along all sad and sober, calling me a martyr to the cause. Then me in the hearse pulled by six horses, going clack, clack, clack over the cobblestones. It fair shakes a body's teeth out of their sockets! The crowd follow on behind.

Everything's black, and not just the dark in the coffin. The mourners are wearing black, men with black crape round their top hats, women sniffing on black handkerchieves under black veils. The horses have plumes of black ostrich feathers. All the coaches are black. There's a cloth of black silk over the coffin, black satin inside.

All in all, I'm quite comfortable. I didn't want to die and leave my Mary, but there was far worse than this in life. The disease that killed me was bad. Coughing and choking on my own blood. Lungs turned to jelly. The white plague they call it, tuberculosis. That was from Northallerton lock-up. I was five weeks on the treadmill, treated like an animal.

They sent me to prison because I fought for my rights, and a vote in elections. The People's Charter. The judge said that was treason, and me a ringleader of traitors. I did throw a grenade or two, and those spiked balls called night cats under the hooves of the cavalry. We'd have blown up the Town Hall, but we were informed on by that scab Allen, the innkeeper from Rotherham, may his soul rot in hell.

I've got a place at the top end of the Cemetery. It would be lovely and restful if everyone would leave me in peace. Harney's giving a speech. What a talker! A lot of the factory lads are shouting drunk, trampling on the flowers and climbing the trees for a better view. It's a shame on the working man.

Well, Mary, we were fighters, but I can't fight any more. Look after the babe. He deserves a better life. All I got was a big funeral.

Strawberry Tongue

Childhood was much more dangerous in the past than it is today. Here is eleven year old Adelaide Green's diary for 17 January, 1854:

I was named Adelaide after a queen, but our house isn't a palace! It's a little brick house in a row of little brick houses, all joined together.

We've got two rooms downstairs and two up. We fetch water from a tap in the street and wash in the kitchen. Our toilet is a smelly privy in the yard that we share with the neighbours.

There are streets and streets of little houses just the same as ours, all puffing out black smoke from coal fires. You can hardly breathe!

When Dad comes home from the workshop, his clothes are covered in dust from the grinding-wheels. That sets us all to coughing. He says one day things will be better, but today my sister Mary died.

I love my sisters. Mary and Emily are three years younger than me. We all sleep in the same bed and I tell them stories every night. They call me "Your Majesty". We're always laughing and joking.

I'm not afraid of dying. Mum says that when children die they go up to Jesus in Heaven. My brother John went to Jesus before I was born. Next were Harriet and George. Then Tom and Sarah. George was the oldest, and he was only five. There must be a lot of room in Heaven.

Dad doesn't earn much money, but he paid for a doctor to see our Mary. The doctor said she had scarlet fever, and that me and Emily had to keep away from her, or we might catch it! We shared Mum and Dad's bed, top to toe.

So we can't say goodbye to our sister. The coffin's in the parlour, and the lid is already nailed down. I want to cry, it's so horrible, but I've got to look after Emily.

Mary's tongue was swollen up like a strawberry, Mum said, and she burned with fever. That was horrible too, but I'm sure Heaven will be nice.

Adelaide herself survived into adulthood, with her sisters Emily and Florence, and her brother Ernest.

Was it my fault?

My name is John Gunson. I'm the engineer in charge of building the dams that give Sheffield its water. Right now, I'm wet, cold and bad-tempered. They say there's a split in the dam wall. Nonsense, of course, but I have to see for myself.

The weather is appalling. Waves on the reservoir are sending spray over the embankment. Mr Craven and Mr Fountain are here. Their men did the actual work on the dam. Mr Swinden of the Sheffield Water Works Company is fussing around. I wish he had stayed at home.

I have to admit, there is a crack, wide enough to put your hand in. It's about fifty metres long, and four metres or so from the top of the wall. Fountain and Swinden have opened the relief valves, but water is coming into the reservoir faster than it is flowing out.

Fountain is shouting, his words snatched away by the wind. 'If we don't relieve the dam of water there'll be a blow up in half an hour!'

I'm so cold, it's hard to think straight. The howling wind gets right inside your head. 'Perhaps you're right!' I shout back to him. 'We'll make a hole in the weir and let it run off.'

Fountain trudges off into the night for gunpowder. Two of his labourers are making a charge hole in the weir. They can hardly see what they are doing. The water level is rising and everything takes so much time.

'Stand clear!' Fountain shouts as he lights the fuse. We all run for cover.

Nothing happens. The man's a fool. I call out, 'I'm going to have another look at the crack and see if you were right! Of course, Swinden insists on coming. The lanterns are flickering and it's infernally dark. But the crack does not seem to have got any worse. I thought so. The wall will hold.

Hell's teeth, I'm standing in water! It's foaming like acid over the top of the embankment and running down into the crack!

'I'm going to check the valve house, Mr Swinden!'

It's the only thing I can do, if I can get down there. The embankment is steep and slippery and I'm almost crawling on hands and knees.

'Come away, Mr Gunson!' Swinden frets. 'You are in grave danger!'

Water is gushing over my head! The wall is breached! 'It's all up,' I yell, 'the embankment is going!'

As we run for our lives there is a tremendous 'Boom!' I stop in confusion. 'What's that, Mr Swinden? What's happening?'

He pulls me by the arm. 'The powder has blown. Too late!'

Swinden drags me off the embankment. My head is reeling. The dam is bursting. My dam. Years of work destroyed in an instant. I hardly know where I am.

There it goes! Where we were standing a moment before, earth and rock tossed aside by a roaring avalanche of water!

'You have saved my life, Mr Swinden,' I croak.

Then I think of all those poor souls down the valley, upon whom I have unleashed this monster, and in the rain I taste salt tears.

Flood Disaster!

'The flood is coming!'

The desperate shout echoed down the Loxley valley at midnight on March 11, 1864. Dale Dyke dam at Bradfield had burst, and seven hundred million gallons of water were thundering down upon the city of Sheffield, devastating everything in its path.

Trees were uprooted and swept along with rocks weighing many tons. Bridges and buildings disappeared, leaving only deep holes gouged by the water. Drowned horses, cattle, pigs – and people – were carried miles from their homes.

Joseph Ibbotson of Bradfield said, 'Language cannot convey any just description of the awful thundering, crashing roar of the torrent. It was as if the earth itself was being rent asunder...'

Imagine the terror of that dark night. The water was cold, and smelled, someone said, 'like a newly-open grave'.

Joseph Dawson said, 'I had carried my wife and my child about twenty yards from the door when the flood met us and knocked us both down... My wife said, "Turn back again to the house." I did so, and just as I got to the door the flood caught us again, and washed my child away...'

The Gannon family climbed onto the roof of their cottage. The flood continued to increase, till it rose to the top of the house, lifted it up, and carried John, Sarah, William, Henry, Peter, Margaret and Emma away...

The torrent of water drowned or dashed to pieces 238 people. Many were children.

Sugar and Spice

Have you got a sweet tooth? The Americans call sweets candy. Sheffield children call them spice.

Some sweets are made from liquorice, and sugar, of course! George Bassett of Sheffield is famous for them. This is how the liquorice department of his factory was described in Victorian times:

In the liquorice department a number of men are engaged in transforming the black extract of liquorice into the shapes in which it is presented in the windows of the confectioners' shops. The extract reaches the works in large black masses. After undergoing the process of boiling and purifying in a steam pan, in one of the rooms on the ground floor, it is hoisted to the rooms above by means of a crane. Portions of this mass, while in a soft state, are then weighed off, and rolled into Spanish juice sticks, or moulded into Pontefract cakes, or propelled through a brass cylinder with steam power into pipes.

The Bassett factory was one of the first to use steam-powered machines. They made many different kinds of liquorice sweet, and sold them to shops that, in turn, sold them to the public.

One day in 1889, salesman Charlie Thompson had an accident that changed the world of sweets for ever.

'Our little nipper kept us up half the night with the colic. The sound of the missus walking up and down with him on her shoulder kept me awake. So I was bleary eyed and clumsy when I got to my first call that morning. Sales were down and I was keen to make a good impression. After all, I'm only paid for what I sell.

I fetched out my liquorice samples, a box of cubes, a box of coconut chips, others of buttons, plugs and cream rocks. Each sort has a name. Each came in its own box and was sold on its own.

Mr Dewsbury was a good customer and my hands were shaking. What did I do but spill the lot! All over the counter! Black ones, pink ones, striped ones and bobbled ones. Square ones and round ones, thick ones and thin ones, straight ones and twisted ones. All mixed up. It was a disaster!

"I'm so sorry!" I scrabbled to sort out the mess.

"Hang on, Charlie!" said Mr Dewsbury. "You've got summat here. They look so pretty, all sorts together. I could sell 'em like this!"

And he did too, lots and lots of them. And when other shops saw what he was doing, they wanted all sorts together, as well. When we came to give them a name, it just had to be Liquorice Allsorts.

Today, sixty million Allsorts are made every week. They are one of the most popular sweets in the world.

Brothers in Bother

I met William and Thomas down by the Wicker. We went to see the arch what's fallen down. I often play with Will. He's eleven, like me. Tom is sixteen, but he follows us around all the time.

We couldn't see much from where we was. 'Let's cross the river!' says Will. He's game for anything, is Will.

Tom whinged. 'Dad told us not, William! He'll take his belt to us!'

We laughed and poked fun. Called him a sissy and worse. I'm sorry now, but Tom spoils all our games. He's afraid of everything.

The first time we went down to the Don, the watchman saw us. We went off and come back, but he saw us again. 'B****r off, you silly little b*****s!' he shouted.

If he hadn't have shouted, we would've gone home. But after that, it were a challenge to beat him.

Someone called him away. Quick as a flash, Will jumped in the water and told us to follow. Now that it come to it, I wasn't so sure. The river was fast and the stones were slippy.

Will, he skipped across and back, twice, while we was looking. 'Come on, Tom,' he says.

'You hold my hand and don't let go!' says Tom.

'I'll wait for you to get across,' says I.

They went very careful, sideways, like crabs. Tom was shaking with fear and holding tight onto Will. They got to the middle of the river.

A man come past me and starts crossing behind them. He was impatient that they were so slow. 'Get a move on!' I heard him say.

That was when Tom slipped. He tottered this way and that, clutching onto Will. He was so big, and Will was so small! He screamed as he fell into the water and Will was jerked in after, like a conker on a string.

The river swallowed them up. I never knew it were so deep. The only thing left was their caps, floating on the water.

The bodies of William and Thomas were found about sixty metres downstream.

Bear

Does a bear have a soul? This is something I often think about as I sit in my cage watching the shadow of the bars creep across the floor.

The workings of the cage are wonderful indeed. It orders and gives meaning to everything in life.

When the shadow of the third bar reaches the big knot-hole in the planking, I meditate quietly by myself. This is when I try to solve the great mysteries. Why did the cage make me? Did it make other bears? Is gluttony a sin?

When the fourth bar reaches the big knot-hole, Youdan makes an offering to the cage and I eat it. Every day I tell myself, Today will be different. I will resist temptation. Every day my stomach over-rules my brain, and I steal the offering and eat it.

Youdan never objects. I suppose he feels that he has done his part in the ceremony. He is a simple fellow, but can be taught a number of useful tricks.

He can, for example, make beautiful sounds on a wooden flute. I rear up and turn on the spot to keep him playing. His repertoire is limited, however, and I have been praying to the cage that he learn another tune.

Sometimes we have a special service in praise of the cage. I dress in a ceremonial skirt and lead Youdan by a chain from the hand to a place of bright lights and many other youdans. They adore me, with ooh and ahh!

Then I dance to the cage while Youdan, my youdan, plays his flute. The other youdans strike hand against hand in a primitive rhythm. It is all very moving, but in the middle of a pirouette I find myself wondering. When I cannot see the cage how do I know that it still exists? What is existence?

I am beset with doubts, a crisis of faith. Do I have a soul? The youdans clearly do not. They exist only to serve. Only I have been chosen by the cage. It is such a heavy burden!

Thomas Youdan kept a Swedish brown bear in the 1860s. He ran a wonderful palace of entertainment in Sheffield called the Surrey Theatre. As well as being a theatre, this had a bar, a ballroom for dancing, and a concert hall for music. It had a museum of curiosities from around the world, with models of cities, Indian and Chinese weapons, and rare stuffed animals. There was a menagerie of live animals, including wolves, huskies, a cockatoo, and the bear.

The theatre burned down in 1865. Fires in theatres were very common before electric lighting because they were lit by candles or, later, gas lamps. It is not known what happened to the bear. Did he go to heaven?

A Cold Grave

In the Sheffield Daily Independent of 2 December, 1902 was a report about Ashantee Natives in Sheffield. The newspaper said, 'The natives, a fine-looking set of people, are to be seen, during the time the entertainment is open to the public, engaged in their different trades, in cooking, or performing some of the quaint ceremonies peculiar to their country.'

Chief Nothei welcomed the visitors, the newspaper continued, 'sat in a wicker-work chair, whilst men and girls went through fantastic dances to the accompaniment of weird music from a number of curious drums, iron castanets and mallets.

A walk round the village cannot fail to be of interest. In front of a number of huts is arranged an African Bazaar. The first attraction is the workshop of the goldsmith, where clever natives may be seen engraving gold and silver rings and bracelets and ornaments.

Their method of preparing potatoes is hardly savoury to the English idea. After boiling the tubers they place them in a kind of tub, which they call a "hadrutchoe", and the women pound them into a fermented mess with a great heavy stick termed in the native tongue the "hadrutchoe mli bi". Potatoes, it should be stated, are the best obtainable equivalent for the yam.'

Did the newspaper report tell the whole truth? One Ashantee woman called Yatso had a different story to tell.

'My baby is dead. With joy we named her Kai Akosia. Kai means that she is our third daughter. Akosia means born on a Sunday.

At home, my husband Meusa La is a fisherman. Home is thousands of miles away in Africa. There are no fish here to catch. We live on potatoes and pretend they are yams. Kai Akosia lived only four days in this damp, cold, terrible place.

"Be grateful, Yatso," says Chief Nothei. "Kai Akosia will be buried in the white folks' cemetery with many strange rituals that cannot fail to be of interest."

Chief Nothei is a toady. I have no interest in their fantastic ideas and weird music. If our priest and priestess were not sick on bad potatoes, I would have them perform the ceremonies for my baby.

My people dance and sing, cook and work wood and metal, all to entertain the English pasty-faces, who smile and say, "How clever!" I'd like to wipe the smiles off their faces with my hadrutchoe mli bi.

I'm sick of England. I want to go home.'

Back to Front

Lieutenant Harold Forsdike has no grave in England. He is thought to have died in the First World War at the Battle of the Somme on 1 July, 1916. His brother Leonard wrote home, saying:

'...as to Harold, nobody really knows that he has been killed. As soon as I could get away I set about to find him, or to get news of him, and in the end rode over to see the colonel. All the news I got was that he was last seen to jump into the German trench. All his men were shot down except one, who landed with Harold at the German line. This man was then wounded and saw Harold go into the trench. What happened to him afterwards I cannot say...'

Leonard was being as gentle as he could, but there is no doubt that Harold was killed. His commanding officer said, 'He was a splendid officer, and did his duty fearlessly, and you will be proud to know that he met his death as an officer and a gentleman.'

This was not really a romantic war. Poison gas was used by both sides. Soldiers were made to 'go over the top' of their trenches and to march slowly and steadily towards the enemy machine guns. Those who refused were likely to be executed for mutiny, though many were nervous wrecks from shell-shock.

The attack led by Lieutenant Forsdike was typical in that so many were killed and so little was gained. Nevertheless, Leonard says:

'In any case, I am proud of him, and I hope you will be, for nobody knows what we all went through, and the magnificent way he led his men over open ground.'

Many thousands died whose bodies were never found. Exploding shells threw earth over the fallen of both sides. Many who were recovered could not be identified. That is why cemeteries have monuments to the 'Unknown Soldier'.

> **If I should die, think only this of me:**
> **That there's some corner of a foreign field**
> **That is forever England.**
>
> *Rupert Brooke, 'The Soldier'.*

Murder

My name's Mary Ann Brownhill and I swear to tell the truth or go straight to hell.

I were near Victoria Station with my friend Betty Hancox. I'm from Crosspool and she's from Carver Lane, so we was both a long way from home when we got caught short.

I says to Betty, 'There's a place we can go in the station. I've been with Mam.'

We're little and quick and nobody noticed us on the platform. We won't get into trouble for not having a ticket, will we? If my mam finds out I'd sooner go straight to hell!

There was lots of people in the waiting room. I don't remember anybody in particular, do you, Betty? No, she don't neither. Well, there was lots of people in black capes. All the toffs wear black capes, don't they.

'I'll go first,' I says to Betty, but she's scared on her own so we went together.

'What's this?' I says when we're in there and the door bolted. She don't know. It's no good asking Betty.

We put our feet on it when we sat down. It were just the right size, like one of them things in church. A hassock? Yes, one of them things in church you put your feet on when you're not supposed to.

We never knew there were a body inside, honest! It were only little. We didn't know it were a babby. Is it true that he were cut into little bits?